# THE SCIENCE BEHIND

# Flight

Louise Spilsbury

Chicago, Illinois

**www.capstonepub.com**
Visit our website to find out more information about Heinemann-Raintree books.

**To order:**
☎ Phone 888-454-2279
💻 Visit www.capstonepub.com
 to browse our catalog and order online.

© 2012 Raintree
an imprint of Capstone Global Library, LLC
Chicago, Illinois

Edited by Claire Throp, Megan Cotugno, and Vaarunika Dharmapala
Designed by Steve Mead
Original illustrations © Capstone Global Library Ltd 2012
Illustrations by Oxford Designers & Illustrators
Picture research by Ruth Blair

Originated by Capstone Global Library Ltd
Printed and bound in China by Leo Paper Products Ltd

15 14 13 12 11
10 9 8 7 6 5 4 3 2 1

**Library of Congress Cataloging-in-Publication Data**

Spilsbury, Louise.
 Flight / Louise Spilsbury.
  p. cm.—(The science behind)
 Includes bibliographical references and index.
 ISBN 978-1-4109-4491-7 (hc)—ISBN 978-1-4109-4502-0 (pb) 1. Aeronautics—Juvenile literature 2. Flight—Juvenile literature. I. Title.
 TL547.S715 2012
 629.13—dc23      2011014627

**Acknowledgments**
We would like to thank the following for permission to reproduce photographs: Corbis p. **16** (© Edward Air Force Base—digital/Science Faction); Getty Images pp. **6** (Steve Finn), **22** (Purestock); Shutterstock pp. **4** (© Alice Kirichenko), **5** (© Ivan Cholakov Gostock-dot-net), **5** (© np), **5** (© Carly Rose Hennigan), **5** (© Geanina Bechea), **5** (© Esterio), **7** (© Dennis Donohue), **8** (© Ragnarock), **10** (© a9luha), **12** (© Zurijeta), **14** (© Terry Straehley), **18** (© Anette Linnea Rasmussen), **19** (© rorem), **20** (© Johnny Lye ), **21** (© Andrej Pol), **23** (© Bruce Rolff), **24** (© Ilja Mašík), **25** (© Ramon Berk); U.S. Air Force photo p. **15** (Chief Master Sgt. Gary Emery).

Cover photograph reproduced with permission of Shutterstock (© dani92026).

We would like to thank Nancy Harris for her invaluable help in the preparation of this book.

Every effort has been made to contact copyright holders of any material reproduced in this book. Any omissions will be rectified in subsequent printings if notice is given to the publisher.

# Contents

## Look for these boxes:

**Stay safe**
These boxes tell you how to keep yourself and your friends safe from harm.

**In your day**
These boxes show you how science is a part of your daily life.

**Measure up!**
These boxes give you some fun facts and figures to think about.

Some words appear in bold, **like this**. You can find out what they mean by looking at the green bar at the bottom of the page or in the glossary.

# Up in the Air

What do you know about being up in the air? Have you flown a kite, made a paper airplane, or traveled on a **jumbo jet**?

## What is flight?

Flight is controlled movement through the air. A kite stays in the air because wind pushes it up. You control a kite by pulling on its strings to make it go higher or lower. When a bird flaps its wings, the wings push air downward. This pushes the bird up into the air.

## Flight and forces

Why is it so hard for people to fly? We cannot even stay in the air for long when we jump off the ground. Making a machine that can move people through the air is difficult, too. That is because there are different **forces** acting on it. A force is a push or a pull. To be able to fly, people have to understand and use forces.

**jumbo jet**   large airplane that can carry hundreds of people
**force**   push or pull that makes things move

Do you recognize the things that can fly in this picture? Which of these flying things are made by people?

# Hot-Air Balloons

For hundreds of years, people tried to fly by copying birds. They made wings out of feathers or wood. They flapped these wings as they jumped off bridges or buildings. It did not work. People just fell to the ground!

## Fighting gravity

The problem is that to get up into the air, everything has to fight a **force** called **gravity**. Gravity is the force that pulls you back to the ground every time you jump. The pulling force of gravity is also what gives you **weight**. Your weight is how heavy you are.

Using homemade wings to try to fly is not really flying. It is really just a way to fall over!

**gravity**  force that pulls things down to the ground
**weight**  how heavy something is

# Birds in flight

Birds are very light. Birds also have strong wings to help them fly. People are much heavier than birds. For our size, our arms are not as strong as a bird's wings. This is why we cannot fly by flapping!

Birds get up into the air by flapping their wings. What happens when you flap your arms?

**Stay safe**
Gravity is useful because it holds us on Earth. However, it can be dangerous, too. If you throw something up in the air, it will fall—and it might land on your head!

Helium balloons can float up into the sky.

## Balloons in the sky

Have you seen a helium balloon **float** off into the sky? Things float when they are lighter than air. Air is the mixture of **gases** in the sky. Air has weight because it is pulled toward Earth by gravity, just as we are. Helium is a gas that is lighter than air.

### Stay safe

Tiny pieces of dirt and dust are lightweight and can sometimes float on air. You can see them when sunlight shines into a room. Too much dust can make you cough or sneeze, so remember to keep your room clean.

**float**   move slowly in the water or on the air
**gas**     substance that is neither a solid nor a liquid

# Flying with hot air

Hot air is lighter than cold air, so it floats upward. People use hot air to fly in hot-air balloons. A burner heats air in a giant balloon. When the hot air rises inside the balloon, it takes the balloon up into the air.

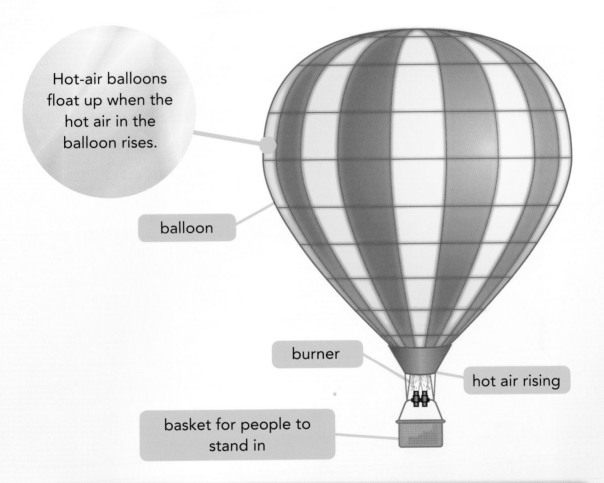

Hot-air balloons float up when the hot air in the balloon rises.

balloon

burner

hot air rising

basket for people to stand in

## In your day

Have you noticed that when you jump into a swimming pool, the deeper water is cooler than water near the top? That is because warm water is lighter than cool water. Warm water rises up, just like hot air.

# Hang Gliders

When you throw a paper airplane, it flies a little, even though it is heavier than air. How does that happen? Planes and **hang gliders** stay in the air because they have wings.

## Wings and lift

Wings provide planes and hang gliders with a **force** called **lift**. Lift is an upward push that comes from the air. The force of lift is opposite to the force of **gravity**. When lift is greater than gravity, a wing goes up into the air. When lift is equal to gravity, it stays at the same level.

This hang glider can fly because it uses the force of lift.

**hang glider**   aircraft similar to a big kite
**lift**   upward push of air on an aircraft or bird as it flies

## How lift works

A wing is curved to create lift. Air blowing over the top of a curved wing has farther to go, so it travels faster than the air below. That means it has less time to press down on the wing from above. Air below the wing has more pushing power than air above, so it pushes the wing upward.

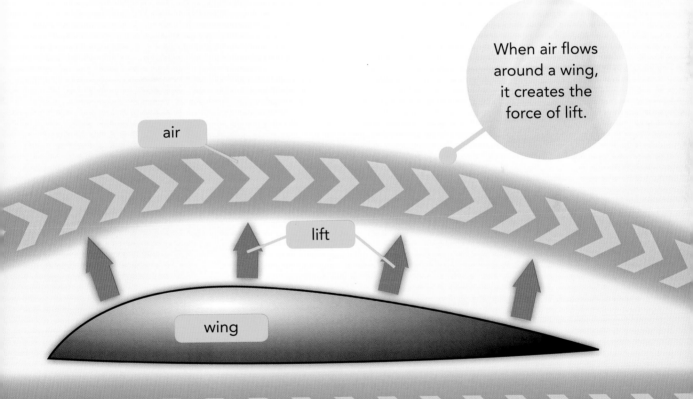

When air flows around a wing, it creates the force of lift.

air

lift

wing

air

What is going to happen to this paper plane after the child lets go of it?

## What a drag!

If wings create lift force, why do paper planes stop flying? Paper planes and hang gliders are slowed down and stopped by another force. This force is called **drag**.

Drag is the force of air that pushes against moving objects. It slows things down or even pushes them backward. When paper planes and hang gliders move through the air, drag pushes against them. When they slow down, air flows more slowly over their wings. This means there is less lift force to fight gravity. When this happens, the paper plane has to land!

**drag** force of air that pushes against objects

## Staying up

Sometimes hang gliders stay up in the air longer by finding a **thermal**. Thermals are areas of warm, rising air. Thermals happen when heat comes off areas of warm land or buildings. This heat warms the air above. The warm air rises and becomes a thermal.

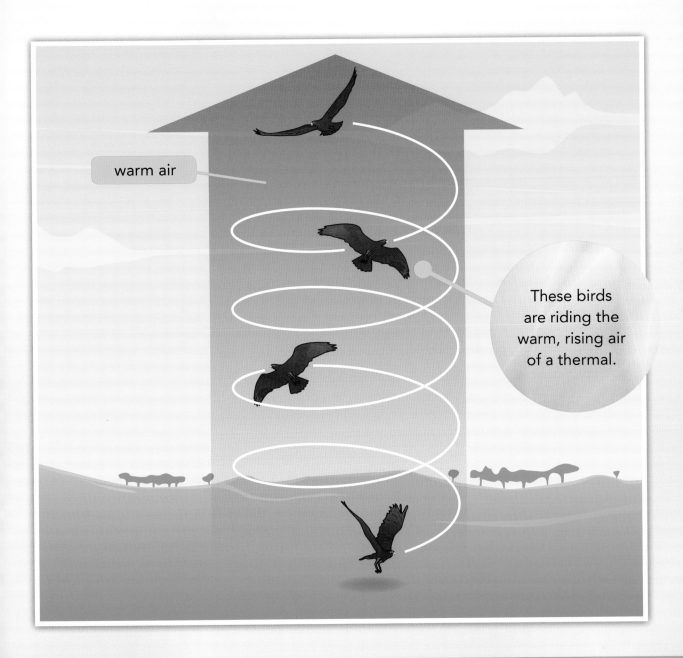

warm air

These birds are riding the warm, rising air of a thermal.

**thermal**    patch of warm air that rises upward

# Airplanes

To make a paper plane fly faster and farther, you can throw it harder. The **force** that moves things forward is called **thrust**. Throwing a paper plane harder gives it more thrust. **Propellers** and engines provide the thrust that airplanes need to move forward.

## Propellers

A propeller is a machine with parts called **blades**. Each blade is shaped like a wing. When an engine makes a propeller spin around and around, the blades create a pulling force. This pulling force helps to pull the plane forward through the air.

Propellers help to move a plane forward.

**Measure up!**
A **jumbo jet** can travel at about 525 miles (845 kilometers) per hour. How far would this jet travel in five hours?

thrust    force that moves an object forward
propeller    machine with two or more metal parts (blades) that turn quickly

## Jet engines

Jet planes make the most of their thrust force by burning **fuel** such as diesel in their engines. When fuel is burned, it makes hot **gases**. These hot gases and air shoot out of the back of the engine. As the gases move backward, they create a thrust force that pushes the plane forward.

Jet engines can make planes fly forward at high speeds.

### In your day
When you blow up a balloon and let it go, air rushes out of the balloon. This pushes the balloon forward through the air. This is similar to the way a jet engine makes thrust!

| | |
|---|---|
| **blade** | metal part shaped like a wing |
| **fuel** | material we use to make heat or power, such as gas, oil, or coal |

There is less drag on streamlined planes, so they can go extremely fast!

## Streamlined planes

Planes need less thrust to move forward if they are **streamlined**. Streamlined planes are long and narrow. There is less **drag** on thinner shapes than wider ones. When you lean down to go faster on a bike, you make yourself a more streamlined shape to reduce drag, too!

### In your day

On a windy day, hold an umbrella open behind you. Its wide shape will cause more drag and slow you down. If you close the umbrella, there will be less drag.

**streamlined**   having a smooth, slim shape that helps something to move more easily

# Thrust and drag

When a plane's engines slow down, there is less thrust. So planes slow down or stop. Pilots also slow planes down by increasing the drag on them. By opening flat pieces of metal called **flaps** on top of the wings, the plane becomes wider. This increases the area that drag pushes against, and it slows the plane down.

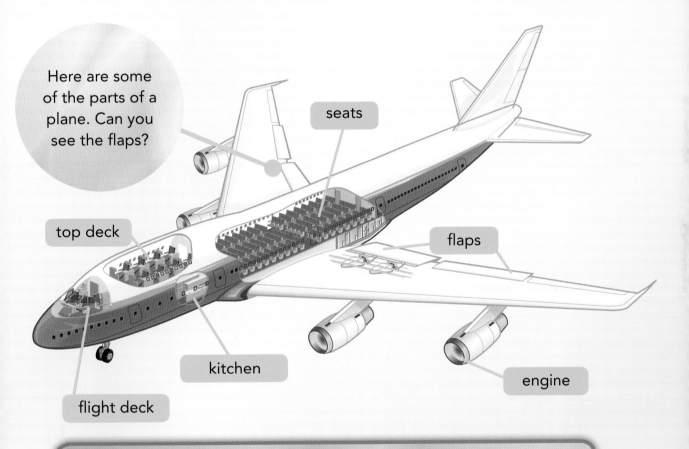

Here are some of the parts of a plane. Can you see the flaps?

seats

top deck

flaps

kitchen

engine

flight deck

## Stay safe

Streamlined shapes can help you, too. When you jump into a pool, make your body narrow by diving in. If you fall flat on your stomach you will do a belly flop, which hurts!

**flap**   movable piece of metal on an aircraft wing that moves in the same way a bird moves its wings

# Helicopters

Stretch out your arms and hold them still while you spin around in one spot. This is like what a helicopter does to take off! Your body is like the helicopter's **rotor**. The rotor spins to turn the helicopter **blades**.

## Straight up!

To leave the ground, planes drive fast down a long strip of land called a runway. This makes air flow quickly over their wings and creates **lift**. A helicopter flies straight up into the air. When a rotor turns the helicopter blades, they throw air downward. This creates the lift the helicopter needs to fly upward.

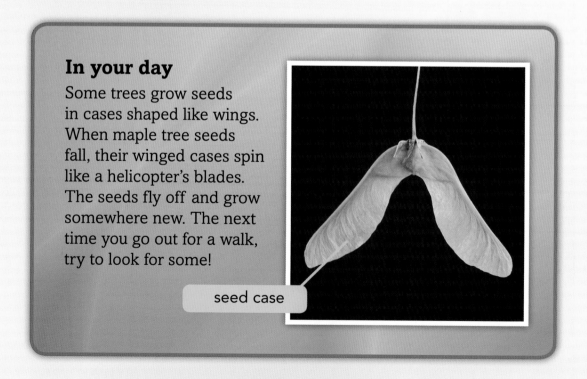

### In your day

Some trees grow seeds in cases shaped like wings. When maple tree seeds fall, their winged cases spin like a helicopter's blades. The seeds fly off and grow somewhere new. The next time you go out for a walk, try to look for some!

seed case

**rotor**    part of a machine, such as a helicopter, that turns around a central point

## How rotors work

A helicopter rotor has four blades. Each blade is shaped like a wing. When the rotor spins, air flows over the top of the blades. The blades push the air down toward the ground. When this air is pushed downward, the rotor and the helicopter are pulled upward.

The rotor blades on a helicopter push air down. Then the helicopter goes up!

helicopter goes up

blades

air pushed down

## Tilting the rotor

During takeoff, a helicopter rotor is straight. In the air, pilots tilt the rotor to make the helicopter fly in different directions. By tilting the rotor, most of the lift **force** still pushes up. However, some of it also pushes forward, left, right, or down. This pushes the helicopter in different directions, too.

### Stay safe

Any spinning blades are very dangerous. When people get into a helicopter when the rotor is spinning, they duck down for safety. In the kitchen, never touch the spinning blades of a blender.

# Hovering helicopters

Helicopters can take off and land in places planes cannot, such as rooftops or hillsides. Helicopters can also stay in one place in the air. This is called **hovering**. Helicopters can hover when the blades turn at a certain speed and the lift force pulling up is the same as the force of **gravity** pulling down.

Rescue helicopters can hover in the air and lift people to safety.

# Spacecraft

Rocket fireworks fly straight up in the air because they contain **gunpowder**. Gunpowder burns when someone sets fire to it. When gunpowder burns, it makes hot **gases**. When the gases shoot downward, the firework shoots straight up!

Spacecraft work in a similar way. They also burn **fuel** to blast hot gases from their tail end. To get into space, they need much more **thrust** than other flying machines. Spacecraft engines are the biggest in the world and reach very fast speeds.

Up, up, and away! This spacecraft is using thrust to fly up into the air.

**gunpowder**   powder that explodes when someone sets fire to it

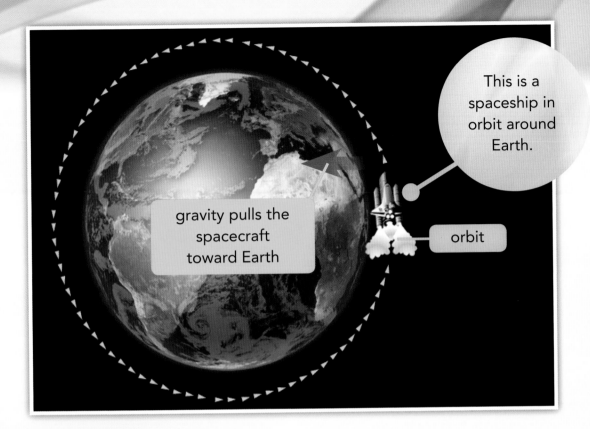

This is a spaceship in orbit around Earth.

gravity pulls the spacecraft toward Earth

orbit

## In orbit

There is no air in space, so there is no **drag** to slow down a spacecraft. It keeps moving. If a spacecraft's movement forward equals the pull of **gravity** downward, it keeps moving at the same distance around Earth. We call this staying in **orbit**. Astronauts use the engines only to change speed and direction.

### In your day
Tie a ball to a piece of string and whirl it around your head so it makes circles in the air. Your pull on the string is like the pull of gravity keeping a spacecraft in orbit around Earth.

**orbit** curved path an object follows around a planet in space

# Understanding Flight

Now when you throw a paper airplane, you will know there are four **forces** working on it: **thrust**, **drag**, **lift**, and **gravity**. You provide the thrust by throwing the plane. This thrust force fights drag and moves the plane forward. When the plane moves through the air, the wings create lift force to fight the force of gravity.

**In your day**

Try making differently shaped paper airplanes. Planes with streamlined shapes have less drag on them. If you throw them hard, they should fly far and fast!

Here you can see the four forces in action on an airplane.

lift

drag

thrust

gravity

# Different planes

Different planes do different jobs, and they use the four forces in different ways. Some planes are big and heavy because they carry many people or things. Big planes cause drag and go more slowly. They have large engines and large wings to produce lift and thrust to fly.

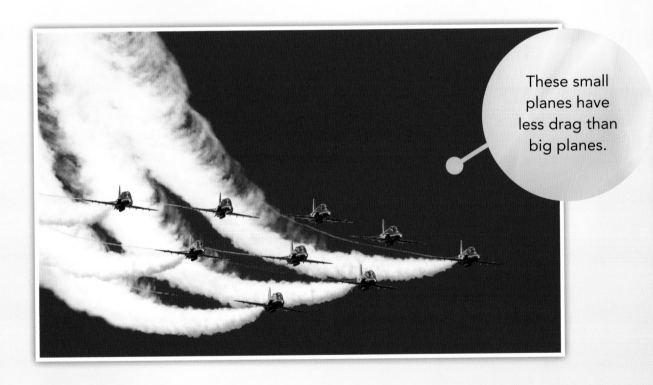

These small planes have less drag than big planes.

Some planes need to move fast and change direction quickly. They are small and thin and only carry one or two people. They are more **streamlined** planes, so they cause less drag. Smaller, narrow wings give them the lift they need. What type of plane would you design?

# Try It Yourself

Make a paper helicopter and test how it flies.

## What you need:

- sheet of paper
- scissors
- paper clips

## What to do:

1. Cut the paper into a rectangle and fold it in half.

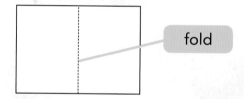

2. Now cut it like this so that it makes a T-shape when you unfold it.

3. Make three more cuts as shown in this picture. Do not cut these too far in.

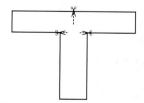

4. Fold one of the top parts of the T-shape back and the other one forward. These are your **blades**. On the upright part of the T-shape, fold both the left and the right part inward. Then attach a paper clip to the bottom.

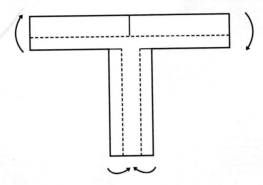

5. Your paper helicopter should look like this when you have finished.

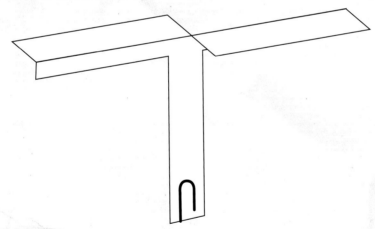

## Try some tests:

What happens if you add two or three paper clips to the bottom? What happens if you fold the wings less far back, so they make more of a Y-shape?

# Glossary

**blade**  metal part shaped like a wing

**drag**  force of air that pushes against objects

**flap**  movable piece of metal on an aircraft wing that moves in the same way a bird moves its wings

**float**  move slowly in the water or on the air

**force**  push or pull that makes things move

**fuel**  material we use to make heat or power, such as gas, oil, or coal

**gas**  substance that is neither a solid nor a liquid

**gravity**  force that pulls things down to the ground

**gunpowder**  powder that explodes when someone sets fire to it

**hang glider**  aircraft similar to a big kite

**hover**  stay in one place in the air

**jumbo jet**  large airplane that can carry hundreds of people

**lift**  upward push of air on an aircraft or bird as it flies

**orbit**  curved path an object follows around a planet in space

**propeller**  machine with two or more metal parts (blades) that turn quickly

**rotor**  part of a machine, such as a helicopter, that turns around a central point

**streamlined**  having a smooth, slim shape that helps something move more easily

**thermal**  patch of warm air that rises upward

**thrust**  force that moves an object forward

**weight**  how heavy something is

# Find Out More

Use these resources to find more fun and useful information about the science behind flight.

## Books

Eason, Sarah. *How Does a Jet Plane Work?* (*How Does It Work?*). New York: Gareth Stevens, 2010.

Jefferis, David. *Planes* (*Extreme Machines*). North Mankato, Minn.: Smart Apple Media, 2008.

Oxlade, Chris. *Planes* (*Transportation Around the World*). Chicago: Heinemann Library, 2008.

Solway, Andrew. *Secrets of Flight* (*Science Secrets*). New York: Marshall Cavendish Benchmark, 2010.

Spilsbury, Richard and Louise. *The Airplane* (*Tales of Invention*). Chicago: Heinemann Library, 2011.

## Websites

**www.nasm.si.edu/exhibitions/gal109/htf/activities/
forcesofflight/web/index.html**
At this exciting website, you can try different wings,
engines, and other parts to see how they affect how
fast and high a plane can fly.

**http://pbskids.org/wayback/flight/index.html**
You can find fun facts about the history of flight at
this website.

**http://quest.nasa.gov/aero/background**
Visit this National Aeronautics and Space
Administration (NASA) website to learn more about the
science of flight.

**www.nasa.gov/audience/forkids/kidsclub/flash/
clubhouse/Lets_Fly_Away.html**
Learn all about the different spacecraft that can fly into
space at this NASA website.

# Index